Teretha's Monthly Budget Tracker

Teretha's
Monthly
Budget
Tracker

Teretha Flowers

XULON PRESS

Xulon Press
2301 Lucien Way #415
Maitland, FL 32751
407.339.4217
www.xulonpress.com

Unless otherwise indicated, Scripture quotations taken from the New King James Version (NKJV). Copyright © 1982 by Thomas Nelson, Inc. Used by permission. All rights reserved.

Printed in the United States of America.

ISBN-13: 978-1-6305-0501-1

TERETHA FLOWERS: INTRODUCTION

According to Average Credit-Card-U-Statistics: <http://www.thebalance.com> The average credit card debt per U.S. household was 8,398 in June 2019. That's $107 trillion in total credit card debt divided by 128 million U.S. households. And according to FDIC: Americans paid banks $113 billion in interest in 2018, up 12% from the $101 billion in interest paid in 2017, and up 49% over the last five years. Finally, <2019 American Household Credit Card Study> In 2019 we estimate the increase in interest paid in the coming to grow, putting Americans on track to pay $122 billion in interest in 2019, an additional $9.6 billion more than the $113 billions currently being paid annually.

Teretha's Simple Monthly Budget Tracker can help you to take charge of your money and financial stability. You will see clearly how much money you have coming in and track where your money is going. It will help you pay your bills on time, help you to cut loose spending, help you to set a budget that can eliminate your credit card debt, and pay loans off early. Teretha's Monthly Budget Tracker will also help you to avoid late fees and cut down interest on loans by paying them off early. To get started on eliminating your debt, first, check you're spending for one month via Bank statement; this will show you where you are spending most of your money. Next, you must focus on paying off the smallest Credit card balance or smallest loan off first. You must be consistent, persistent, and diligent to work on eliminating your debt. Before you know it, bills will be consistently paid on time; you will avoiding late fees, you will have eliminated the debt.

What to do with your extra money? You can take your extra money:

1.) Save it for your retirement
2.) Invest it
3.) Buy a building that will bring you extra income by renting
4.) Apply that extra money toward starting that business you wanted.

Teretha's Monthly Budget Tracker can help you take charge of your life and gain financial stability.

TERETHA'S MONTHLY BUDGET TRACKER

January 20__

This plan can easily help keep you on track to pay your bills on time, make you aware of how much money is coming and going out. This simple monthly tracker can help you pay credit cards off early, and help to cut loose spending.

Paydays: Total _____

01/__/2__: $_____ Tithe/Charity: $_____ Extra Income: $_____ = _____

01/__/2__: $_____ Tithe/Charity: $_____ Extra Income: $_____ = _____

01/__/2__: $_____ Tithe/Charity: $_____ Extra Income: $_____ = _____

01/__/2__: $_____ Tithe/Charity: $_____ Extra Income: $_____ = _____

List the bills that are due between the 1-15th of the month.

Mortgage/Rent: $_____ Due:_____   <u>Miscellaneous Bills</u>

_____: $_____ Due:____   _____: $_____ Due:____

_____: $_____ Due:____   _____: $_____ Due:____

_____: $_____ Due:____   _____: $_____ Due:____

_____: $_____ Due:____   _____: $_____ Due:____

List the bills that are due between the 16-31st of the month. Savings: $_____

Car Note: $_____ Due:_____   <u>Miscellaneous Bills</u>

_____: $_____ Due:_____   _____: $_____ Due:_____

_____: $_____ Due:_____   _____: $_____ Due:_____

_____: $_____ Due:_____   _____: $_____ Due:_____

_____: $_____ Due:_____   _____: $_____ Due:_____

Credit Cards: Saving: $_____

(1.)_____: $_____ Due:_____

(2.)_____: $_____ Due:_____

(3.)_____: $_____ Due:_____

Tickets:

(1.)_____: $_____ Due:_____

(2.)_____: $_____ Due:_____

(3.)_____: $_____ Due:_____

Loans:

(1.)_____: $_____ Due:_____

(2.)_____: $_____ Due:_____

(3.)_____: $_____ Due:_____

Monthly Budget Worksheet:
January 20__:

Tally budget and balance: 1-15

Tally budget and balance: 16-31

Teretha's Monthly Budget Tracker

February 20__

This plan can easily help keep you on track to pay your bills on time, make you aware of how much money is coming and going out. This simple monthly tracker can help you pay credit cards off early, and help to cut loose spending.

Paydays: Total _____

02/__/2__: $_____Tithe/Charity: $_____ Extra Income: $_____ = _____

02/__/2__: $_____Tithe/Charity: $_____ Extra Income: $_____ = _____

02/__/2__: $_____Tithe/Charity: $_____ Extra Income: $_____ = _____

02/__/2__: $_____Tithe/Charity: $_____ Extra Income: $_____ = _____

List the bills that are due between the 1-15th of the month.

Mortgage/Rent: $_____ Due:_____   <u>Miscellaneous Bills</u>

_____: $_____ Due:____   _____: $_____ Due:____

_____: $_____ Due:____   _____: $_____ Due:____

_____: $_____ Due:____   _____: $_____ Due:____

_____: $_____ Due:____   _____: $_____ Due:____

List the bills that are due between the 16-29th of the month. Savings: $_____

Car Note: $_____ Due:_____   <u>Miscellaneous Bills</u>

_____ : $_____ Due:____   _____ : $_____ Due:____

_____ : $_____ Due:____   _____ : $_____ Due:____

_____ : $_____ Due:____   _____ : $_____ Due:____

_____ : $_____ Due:____   _____ : $_____ Due:____

Credit Cards: Saving: $_____

(1.)_____ : $_____ Due:_____

(2.)_____ : $_____ Due:_____

(3.)_____ : $_____ Due:_____

Tickets:

(1.)_____ : $_____ Due:_____

(2.)_____ : $_____ Due:_____

(3.)_____ : $_____ Due:_____

Loans:

(1.)_____ : $_____ Due:_____

(2.)_____ : $_____ Due:_____

(3.)_____ : $_____ Due:_____

Monthly Budget Worksheet:
February 20___:

Tally budget and balance: 1-15

Tally budget and balance: 16-29

Teretha's Monthly Budget Tracker

March 20___

This plan can easily help keep you on track to pay your bills on time, make you aware of how much money is coming and going out. This simple monthly tracker can help you pay credit cards off early, and help to cut loose spending.

Paydays: Total _____

03/___/2___: $_____Tithe/Charity: $_____ Extra Income: $_____ = _____

03/___/2___: $_____Tithe/Charity: $_____ Extra Income: $_____ = _____

03/___/2___: $_____Tithe/Charity: $_____ Extra Income: $_____ = _____

03/___/2___: $_____Tithe/Charity: $_____ Extra Income: $_____ = _____

List the bills that are due between the 1-15th of the month.

Mortgage/Rent: $_____ Due:_____   <u>Miscellaneous Bills</u>

_____: $_____ Due:_____   _____: $_____ Due:_____

_____: $_____ Due:_____   _____: $_____ Due:_____

_____: $_____ Due:_____   _____: $_____ Due:_____

_____: $_____ Due:_____   _____: $_____ Due:_____

List the bills that are due between the 16-31st of the month. Savings: $_____

Car Note: $_____ Due:_____   <u>Miscellaneous Bills</u>

_____: $_____ Due:_____   _____: $_____ Due:_____

_____: $_____ Due:_____   _____: $_____ Due:_____

_____: $_____ Due:_____   _____: $_____ Due:_____

_____: $_____ Due:_____   _____: $_____ Due:_____

Credit Cards: Saving: $_____

(1.)_____: $_____ Due:_____

(2.)_____: $_____ Due:_____

(3.)_____: $_____ Due:_____

Tickets:

(1.)_____: $_____ Due:_____

(2.)_____: $_____ Due:_____

(3.)_____: $_____ Due:_____

Loans:

(1.)_____: $_____ Due:_____

(2.)_____: $_____ Due:_____

(3.)_____: $_____ Due:_____

Monthly Budget Worksheet:
March 20__:

Tally budget and balance: 1-15

Tally budget and balance: 16-31

Teretha's Monthly Budget Tracker

April 20__

This plan can easily help keep you on track to pay your bills on time, make you aware of how much money is coming and going out. This simple monthly tracker can help you pay credit cards off early, and help to cut loose spending.

Paydays: Total _____

04/__/2__: $_____Tithe/Charity: $_____ Extra Income: $_____ = _____

04/__/2__: $_____Tithe/Charity: $_____ Extra Income: $_____ = _____

04/__/2__: $_____Tithe/Charity: $_____ Extra Income: $_____ = _____

04/__/2__: $_____Tithe/Charity: $_____ Extra Income: $_____ = _____

List the bills that are due between the 1-15th of the month.

Mortgage/Rent: $_____ Due:_____   <u>Miscellaneous Bills</u>

_____: $_____ Due:_____   _____: $_____ Due:_____

_____: $_____ Due:_____   _____: $_____ Due:_____

_____: $_____ Due:_____   _____: $_____ Due:_____

_____: $_____ Due:_____   _____: $_____ Due:_____

List the bills that are due between the 16-30th of the month. Savings: $_____

Car Note: $_____ Due:_____   <u>Miscellaneous Bills</u>

_____ : $_____ Due:____   _____ : $_____ Due:____

_____ : $_____ Due:____   _____ : $_____ Due:____

_____ : $_____ Due:____   _____ : $_____ Due:____

_____ : $_____ Due:____   _____ : $_____ Due:____

Credit Cards: Saving: $_____

(1.)_____ : $_____ Due:_____

(2.)_____ : $_____ Due:_____

(3.)_____ : $_____ Due:_____

Tickets:

(1.)_____ : $_____ Due:_____

(2.)_____ : $_____ Due:_____

(3.)_____ : $_____ Due:_____

Loans:

(1.)_____ : $_____ Due:_____

(2.)_____ : $_____ Due:_____

(3.)_____ : $_____ Due:_____

Monthly Budget Worksheet:
April 20__:

Tally budget and balance: 1-15

Tally budget and balance: 16-30

Teretha's Monthly Budget Tracker

May 20__

This plan can easily help keep you on track to pay your bills on time, make you aware of how much money is coming and going out. This simple monthly tracker can help you pay credit cards off early, and help to cut loose spending.

Paydays: Total _____

05/__/2__: $_____Tithe/Charity: $_____ Extra Income: $_____ = _____

05/__/2__: $_____Tithe/Charity: $_____ Extra Income: $_____ = _____

05/__/2__: $_____Tithe/Charity: $_____ Extra Income: $_____ = _____

05/__/2__: $_____Tithe/Charity: $_____ Extra Income: $_____ = _____

List the bills that are due between the 1-15th of the month.

Mortgage/Rent: $_____ Due:_____   <u>Miscellaneous Bills</u>

_____: $_____ Due:____   _____: $_____ Due:____

_____: $_____ Due:____   _____: $_____ Due:____

_____: $_____ Due:____   _____: $_____ Due:____

_____: $_____ Due:____   _____: $_____ Due:____

List the bills that are due between the 16-31st of the month. Savings: $_____

Car Note: $_____ Due:_____   Miscellaneous Bills

_____: $_____ Due:_____   _____: $_____ Due:_____

_____: $_____ Due:_____   _____: $_____ Due:_____

_____: $_____ Due:_____   _____: $_____ Due:_____

_____: $_____ Due:_____   _____: $_____ Due:_____

Credit Cards: Saving: $_____

(1.)_____: $_____ Due:_____

(2.)_____: $_____ Due:_____

(3.)_____: $_____ Due:_____

Tickets:

(1.)_____: $_____ Due:_____

(2.)_____: $_____ Due:_____

(3.)_____: $_____ Due:_____

Loans:

(1.)_____: $_____ Due:_____

(2.)_____: $_____ Due:_____

(3.)_____: $_____ Due:_____

Monthly Budget Worksheet:
May 20__:

Tally budget and balance: 1-15

Tally budget and balance: 16-31

Teretha's Monthly Budget Tracker

June 20__

This plan can easily help keep you on track to pay your bills on time, make you aware of how much money is coming and going out. This simple monthly tracker can help you pay credit cards off early, and help to cut loose spending.

Paydays: Total _____

06/__/2__: $_____Tithe/Charity: $_____ Extra Income: $_____ = _____

06/__/2__: $_____Tithe/Charity: $_____ Extra Income: $_____ = _____

06/__/2__: $_____Tithe/Charity: $_____ Extra Income: $_____ = _____

06/__/2__: $_____Tithe/Charity: $_____ Extra Income: $_____ = _____

List the bills that are due between the 1-15th of the month.

Mortgage/Rent: $_____ Due:_____   Miscellaneous Bills

_____: $_____ Due:____   _____: $_____ Due:____

_____: $_____ Due:____   _____: $_____ Due:____

_____: $_____ Due:____   _____: $_____ Due:____

_____: $_____ Due:____   _____: $_____ Due:____

List the bills that are due between the 16-30th of the month. Savings: $_____

Car Note: $_____ Due:_____   <u>Miscellaneous Bills</u>

_____: $_____ Due:____   _____: $_____ Due:____

_____: $_____ Due:____   _____: $_____ Due:____

_____: $_____ Due:____   _____: $_____ Due:____

_____: $_____ Due:____   _____: $_____ Due:____

Credit Cards: Saving: $_____

(1.)_____: $_____ Due:_____

(2.)_____: $_____ Due:_____

(3.)_____: $_____ Due:_____

Tickets:

(1.)_____: $_____ Due:_____

(2.)_____: $_____ Due:_____

(3.)_____: $_____ Due:_____

Loans:

(1.)_____: $_____ Due:_____

(2.)_____: $_____ Due:_____

(3.)_____: $_____ Due:_____

Monthly Budget Worksheet:
June 20__:

Tally budget and balance: 1-15

Tally budget and balance: 16-30

Teretha's Monthly Budget Tracker

July 20__

This plan can easily help keep you on track to pay your bills on time, make you aware of how much money is coming and going out. This simple monthly tracker can help you pay credit cards off early, and help to cut loose spending.

Paydays: Total _____

07/__/2__: $_____Tithe/Charity: $_____ Extra Income: $_____ = _____

07/__/2__: $_____Tithe/Charity: $_____ Extra Income: $_____ = _____

07/__/2__: $_____Tithe/Charity: $_____ Extra Income: $_____ = _____

07/__/2__: $_____Tithe/Charity: $_____ Extra Income: $_____ = _____

List the bills that are due between the 1-15th of the month.

Mortgage/Rent: $_____ Due:_____   Miscellaneous Bills

_____: $_____ Due:_____   _____: $_____ Due:_____

_____: $_____ Due:_____   _____: $_____ Due:_____

_____: $_____ Due:_____   _____: $_____ Due:_____

_____: $_____ Due:_____   _____: $_____ Due:_____

List the bills that are due between the 16-31st of the month. Savings: $_____

Car Note: $_____ Due:_____   <u>Miscellaneous Bills</u>

_____: $_____ Due:____   _____: $_____ Due:____

_____: $_____ Due:____   _____: $_____ Due:____

_____: $_____ Due:____   _____: $_____ Due:____

_____: $_____ Due:____   _____: $_____ Due:____

Credit Cards: Saving: $_____

(1.)_____: $_____ Due:_____

(2.)_____: $_____ Due:_____

(3.)_____: $_____ Due:_____

Tickets:

(1.)_____: $_____ Due:_____

(2.)_____: $_____ Due:_____

(3.)_____: $_____ Due:_____

Loans:

(1.)_____: $_____ Due:_____

(2.)_____: $_____ Due:_____

(3.)_____: $_____ Due:_____

Monthly Budget Worksheet:
July 20___:

Tally budget and balance: 1-15

Tally budget and balance: 16-31

Teretha's Monthly Budget Tracker

August 20__

This plan can easily help keep you on track to pay your bills on time, make you aware of how much money is coming and going out. This simple monthly tracker can help you pay credit cards off early, and help to cut loose spending.

Paydays: Total _____

08/__/2__: $_____Tithe/Charity: $_____ Extra Income: $_____ = _____

08/__/2__: $_____Tithe/Charity: $_____ Extra Income: $_____ = _____

08/__/2__: $_____Tithe/Charity: $_____ Extra Income: $_____ = _____

08/__/2__: $_____Tithe/Charity: $_____ Extra Income: $_____ = _____

List the bills that are due between the 1-15th of the month.

Mortgage/Rent: $_____ Due:_____   Miscellaneous Bills

_____: $_____ Due:_____   _____: $_____ Due:_____

_____: $_____ Due:_____   _____: $_____ Due:_____

_____: $_____ Due:_____   _____: $_____ Due:_____

_____: $_____ Due:_____   _____: $_____ Due:_____

List the bills that are due between the 16-31st of the month. Savings: $_____

Car Note: $_____ Due:_____   <u>Miscellaneous Bills</u>

_____: $_____ Due:____   _____: $_____ Due:____

_____: $_____ Due:____   _____: $_____ Due:____

_____: $_____ Due:____   _____: $_____ Due:____

_____: $_____ Due:____   _____: $_____ Due:____

Credit Cards: Saving: $_____

(1.)_____: $_____ Due:_____

(2.)_____: $_____ Due:_____

(3.)_____: $_____ Due:_____

Tickets:

(1.)_____: $_____ Due:_____

(2.)_____: $_____ Due:_____

(3.)_____: $_____ Due:_____

Loans:

(1.)_____: $_____ Due:_____

(2.)_____: $_____ Due:_____

(3.)_____: $_____ Due:_____

Monthly Budget Worksheet:
August 20__:

Tally budget and balance: 1-15

Tally budget and balance: 16-31

Teretha's Monthly Budget Tracker

September 20__

This plan can easily help keep you on track to pay your bills on time, make you aware of how much money is coming and going out. This simple monthly tracker can help you pay credit cards off early, and help to cut loose spending.

Paydays: Total _____

09/__/2__: $_____ Tithe/Charity: $_____ Extra Income: $_____ = _____

09/__/2__: $_____ Tithe/Charity: $_____ Extra Income: $_____ = _____

09/__/2__: $_____ Tithe/Charity: $_____ Extra Income: $_____ = _____

09/__/2__: $_____ Tithe/Charity: $_____ Extra Income: $_____ = _____

List the bills that are due between the 1-15th of the month.

Mortgage/Rent: $_____ Due:_____   <u>Miscellaneous Bills</u>

_____: $_____ Due:_____   _____: $_____ Due:_____

_____: $_____ Due:_____   _____: $_____ Due:_____

_____: $_____ Due:_____   _____: $_____ Due:_____

_____: $_____ Due:_____   _____: $_____ Due:_____

List the bills that are due between the 16-30th of the month. Savings: $_____

Car Note: $_____ Due:_____   <u>Miscellaneous Bills</u>

_____: $_____ Due:____   _____: $_____ Due:____

_____: $_____ Due:____   _____: $_____ Due:____

_____: $_____ Due:____   _____: $_____ Due:____

_____: $_____ Due:____   _____: $_____ Due:____

Credit Cards: Saving: $_____

(1.)_____: $_____ Due:_____

(2.)_____: $_____ Due:_____

(3.)_____: $_____ Due:_____

Tickets:

(1.)_____: $_____ Due:_____

(2.)_____: $_____ Due:_____

(3.)_____: $_____ Due:_____

Loans:

(1.)_____: $_____ Due:_____

(2.)_____: $_____ Due:_____

(3.)_____: $_____ Due:_____

Monthly Budget Worksheet:
September 20__:

Tally budget and balance: 1-15

Tally budget and balance: 16-30

Teretha's Monthly Budget Tracker

October 20__

This plan can easily help keep you on track to pay your bills on time, make you aware of how much money is coming and going out. This simple monthly tracker can help you pay credit cards off early, and help to cut loose spending.

Paydays: Total _____

10/__/2__: $_____Tithe/Charity: $_____ Extra Income: $_____ = _____

10/__/2__: $_____Tithe/Charity: $_____ Extra Income: $_____ = _____

10/__/2__: $_____Tithe/Charity: $_____ Extra Income: $_____ = _____

10/__/2__: $_____Tithe/Charity: $_____ Extra Income: $_____ = _____

List the bills that are due between the 1-15th of the month.

Mortgage/Rent: $_____ Due:_____   Miscellaneous Bills

_____: $_____ Due:_____   _____: $_____ Due:_____

_____: $_____ Due:_____   _____: $_____ Due:_____

_____: $_____ Due:_____   _____: $_____ Due:_____

_____: $_____ Due:_____   _____: $_____ Due:_____

List the bills that are due between the 16-31st of the month. Savings: $_____

Car Note: $_____ Due:_____   <u>Miscellaneous Bills</u>

_____: $_____ Due:____   _____: $_____ Due:____

_____: $_____ Due:____   _____: $_____ Due:____

_____: $_____ Due:____   _____: $_____ Due:____

_____: $_____ Due:____   _____: $_____ Due:____

Credit Cards: Saving: $_____

(1.)_____: $_____ Due:_____

(2.)_____: $_____ Due:_____

(3.)_____: $_____ Due:_____

Tickets:

(1.)_____: $_____ Due:_____

(2.)_____: $_____ Due:_____

(3.)_____: $_____ Due:_____

Loans:

(1.)_____: $_____ Due:_____

(2.)_____: $_____ Due:_____

(3.)_____: $_____ Due:_____

Monthly Budget Worksheet:
October 20__:

Tally budget and balance: 1-15

Tally budget and balance: 16-31

Teretha's Monthly Budget Tracker

November 20__

This plan can easily help keep you on track to pay your bills on time, make you aware of how much money is coming and going out. This simple monthly tracker can help you pay credit cards off early, and help to cut loose spending.

Paydays: Total _____

11/__/2__: $_____ Tithe/Charity: $_____ Extra Income: $_____ = _____

11/__/2__: $_____ Tithe/Charity: $_____ Extra Income: $_____ = _____

11/__/2__: $_____ Tithe/Charity: $_____ Extra Income: $_____ = _____

11/__/2__: $_____ Tithe/Charity: $_____ Extra Income: $_____ = _____

List the bills that are due between the 1-15th of the month.

Mortgage/Rent: $_____ Due:_____   Miscellaneous Bills

_____: $_____ Due:____   _____: $_____ Due:____

_____: $_____ Due:____   _____: $_____ Due:____

_____: $_____ Due:____   _____: $_____ Due:____

_____: $_____ Due:____   _____: $_____ Due:____

List the bills that are due between the 16-30th of the month. Savings: $_____

Car Note: $_____ Due:_____   <u>Miscellaneous Bills</u>

_____: $_____ Due:_____   _____: $_____ Due:_____

_____: $_____ Due:_____   _____: $_____ Due:_____

_____: $_____ Due:_____   _____: $_____ Due:_____

_____: $_____ Due:_____   _____: $_____ Due:_____

Credit Cards: Saving: $_____

(1.)_____: $_____ Due:_____

(2.)_____: $_____ Due:_____

(3.)_____: $_____ Due:_____

Tickets:

(1.)_____: $_____ Due:_____

(2.)_____: $_____ Due:_____

(3.)_____: $_____ Due:_____

Loans:

(1.)_____: $_____ Due:_____

(2.)_____: $_____ Due:_____

(3.)_____: $_____ Due:_____

Monthly Budget Worksheet:
November 20__:

Tally budget and balance: 1-15

Tally budget and balance: 16-30

TERETHA'S MONTHLY BUDGET TRACKER

December 20__

This plan can easily help keep you on track to pay your bills on time, make you aware of how much money is coming and going out. This simple monthly tracker can help you pay credit cards off early, and help to cut loose spending.

Paydays: Total _____

12/__/2__: $_____Tithe/Charity: $_____ Extra Income: $_____ = _____

12/__/2__: $_____Tithe/Charity: $_____ Extra Income: $_____ = _____

12/__/2__: $_____Tithe/Charity: $_____ Extra Income: $_____ = _____

12/__/2__: $_____Tithe/Charity: $_____ Extra Income: $_____ = _____

List the bills that are due between the 1-15th of the month.

Mortgage/Rent: $_____ Due:_____   Miscellaneous Bills

_____: $_____ Due:_____   _____: $_____ Due:_____

_____: $_____ Due:_____   _____: $_____ Due:_____

_____: $_____ Due:_____   _____: $_____ Due:_____

_____: $_____ Due:_____   _____: $_____ Due:_____

List the bills that are due between the 16-31st of the month. Savings: $_____

Car Note: $_____ Due:_____   <u>Miscellaneous Bills</u>

_____: $_____ Due:____   _____: $_____ Due:____

_____: $_____ Due:____   _____: $_____ Due:____

_____: $_____ Due:____   _____: $_____ Due:____

_____: $_____ Due:____   _____: $_____ Due:____

Credit Cards: Saving: $_____

(1.)_____: $_____ Due:_____

(2.)_____: $_____ Due:_____

(3.)_____: $_____ Due:_____

Tickets:

(1.)_____: $_____ Due:_____

(2.)_____: $_____ Due:_____

(3.)_____: $_____ Due:_____

Loans:

(1.)_____: $_____ Due:_____

(2.)_____: $_____ Due:_____

(3.)_____: $_____ Due:_____

Monthly Budget Worksheet:
December 20__:

Tally budget and balance: 1-15

Tally budget and balance: 16-31